Jhansi & Rohit
Aug 2020

PUFFIN BOOKS

FUN IN DEVLOK OMNIBUS

Dr Devdutt Pattanaik studied medicine but decided he loves telling stories better. He feels stories are like Eclair sweets; if you chew long enough, you get a burst of the chocolate that is locked inside. So rather than working as a doctor, he decided to write and tell ancient Indian stories and reveal the idea-chocolate within them. He believes these stories are the gifts of our ancestors. He has been doing this for a long time and even uses the wisdom of these stories to help businesses. To know more, visit www.devdutt.com.

Fun in Devlok Omnibus

Devdutt pattanaik

Illustrations by Vishal Tondon

PUFFIN BOOKS

PUFFIN BOOKS

USA | Canada | UK | Ireland | Australia
New Zealand | India | South Africa | China

Puffin Books is part of the Penguin Random House group of
companies whose addresses can be found at global.penguinrandomhouse.com

Published by Penguin Random House India Pvt. Ltd
7th Floor, Infinity Tower C, DLF Cyber City,
Gurgaon 122 002, Haryana, India

Penguin
Random House
India

First published by Penguin Books India 2014

10 9 8 7 6 5 4 3 2

The stories in this series are inspired by various details of Hindu mythology and
do not seek to supplement or substitute the original works.

ISBN 9780143333449

For sale in the Indian Subcontinent only

Typeset in Cochin by Abha Graphics, New Delhi
Printed at Repro Knowledgecast Limited, India

www.penguin.co.in

Contents

Contents

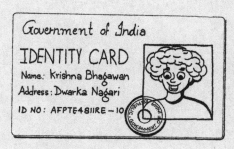

Government of India

IDENTITY CARD

Name: Krishna Bhagawan

Address: Dwarka Nagari

ID NO: AFPTE4811RE-10

An Identity Card for

Krishna

Our story starts in the Mumbai airport, a place where aeroplanes come and go. They come from various cities and they go to various cities, carrying hundreds of passengers and their luggage. There are huge television screens telling people which flights are arriving and which flights are departing, which flights are on time and which flights are delayed. There are thousands of people inside the

building, and as many outside. It's a
really crowded place!

One day, a handsome young man,
who looked about seventeen years

    An Identity Card for Krishna

old, came to this airport. His skin was very dark and his eyes were very bright. He had curly hair and a gentle smile on his lips. He wore a bright yellow T-shirt and faded blue jeans. He carried no luggage, just a tiny backpack. He looked very relaxed and seemed rather charming.

The young man noticed that everyone around was rather worried. They were carrying bags, moving trolleys, checking their tickets, bidding farewell to their family and friends, confirming flight timings and wondering if there was enough time for a snack before they had to board the plane.

'Eh, where are you going?' snarled the security guard at the airport gate. It

was Mr Jayaramakrishnan Murthy, a giant of a man, with a big moustache and a bigger belly. Actually, Mr Jayaramakrishnan Murthy was not as tough as he looked. He was secretly afraid of lizards, but no one except his wife, Mrs Ananda Murthy, knew this.

Like all guards, Mr Murthy looked at everyone suspiciously. It was his job. Everyone was a suspected troublemaker until they proved they were not. And to prove that one is not a troublemaker one had to show Mr Murthy one's ticket and one's identity card. Only then would Mr Murthy let you into the airport.

GOVT OF MAHARASHTRA
DRIVERS LICENSE
Name: Sunil Kumar
Age: 18 years
Address: 23/8, 16th Road
Khar, Mumbai

TAX D
PAN CA
Name: Mrs Srimati
Age: 30 years
Address: A-11, Lajpat Nagar
Delhi, India

TRIPLUS CHEMICALS L
IDENTITY CARD
Employee: Salim Khan
Designation: Manager
Age: 28 years
Blood Group: AB+ve

Just a few minutes ago, there had been a problem. A man with ten heads had arrived at the gate demanding to be let in. 'Show me your identity card first,' Mr Murthy had snarled.

'Don't you know who I am? There is only one man in this world with ten heads!' yelled the man with ten heads. Mr Murthy, very politely but firmly, said, 'Your identity card, please, sir.' The man with ten heads had no choice but to do as asked. He had shown his identity cards. Not one, but ten. Each of the ten identity cards had his name written in bold letters: Ravan Lankapati.

Mr Murthy had never seen a man with ten heads or a man with ten identity cards, each card claiming he was the same person. 'Why do you not carry one identity card?' said Mr Murthy. 'Because,' explained Ravan Lankapati, rolling his eyes, 'I have ten heads. That's the rule. One identity card for one head. Don't you know that?' Mr Murthy did not know this rule, but he let the strange man with ten heads go in.

Now before him stood this handsome young man with curly hair and yellow T-shirt in the queue waiting patiently for his turn. Unlike other passengers, this man seemed in no hurry to enter the airport. He looked at everyone and everything with great curiosity.

An Identity Card for Krishna

Perhaps this was the first time he was boarding an aeroplane. Perhaps this was the first time he was in an airport. Mr Murthy worked in the airport but had never boarded a plane himself. He had promised himself that before retirement, he and his wife would travel to Tirupati on a plane.

'Well?' said Mr Jayaramakrishnan Murthy waiting for the handsome young man to show his ticket and his identity card.

The youth presented a printout of the ticket. It was a flight from Mumbai to Guwahati via Kolkata, a long, very long flight from the west of India to the east. Mr Murthy searched for the man's name. It was ... Mr Murthy

BOARDING PASS
Name : KRISHNA BHAGAVAN
From : Mumbai   To : Guwahati
PNR NO. G*O*V*I*N*D*O1

Frisking of person and checking of hand baggage

could not believe his eyes. 'Krishna Bhagavan?'

'Yes,' said the young man with a disarming smile. Mr Murthy smiled back. He could not resist asking, 'Which is the name and which is the surname?'

'How does it matter?' replied the young man, his voice soft, almost musical.

'It does not,' said Mr Murthy, starting to like the young man. 'But still I would like to know. But it is okay if you do not want to tell me. May I see your identity card?'

The young man blinked. 'Sorry, why do I need an identity card?' Mr Murthy said, 'To prove who you are. Are you really Krishna Bhagavan?'

'Yes, I am. Don't you recognize me? You see my photo every day in the morning.'

'I do not!' Mr Jayaramakrishnan

Murthy shouted, then added, 'What do you mean?'

'I am the one whose photo hangs on the extreme left of your puja room. I am the one with the cows and the flute.'

Mr Murthy could not believe what the young man was saying. Was this a joke? The number of passengers standing in queue behind the young man wanting to get into the airport terminal had increased. Everyone was starting to get impatient. A young woman at the end of the line shouted, 'If there is a problem with that man's identity card, can you at least let us pass please.'

Mr Murthy instructed his junior to take over his duties while he dealt with 'Krishna Bhagavan'. 'Are you making fun of me?' he asked. 'No,' said Krishna Bhagavan, looking very serious. 'Don't you recognize me? I am the one who you serve butter every morning. You have been serving me butter for twenty-three years.' That was true. Mr Murthy wondered how the young man knew this. Was he who he claimed to be? 'I am so glad I met you. I am on my way to Guwahati

to see another devotee, Lata-kumari. She has been serving me butter every morning for sixty-two years. Now she is old and ill and calling for me. Thought I should pay her a visit.'

The man sounded totally sincere. Mr Murthy wanted to believe him. But this is the real world. Gods do not come to airports in the real world. They exist in photos in puja rooms and inside temples and in storybooks and television serials. But then he remembered the man with ten heads—Ravan Lankapati. What was happening? Mr Murthy felt nervous.

'Listen Mr Bhagavan, I am a policeman. I can arrest you for making fun of an officer of the law.'

'But I am not making fun of you. I am your Krishna,' said the young man, most earnestly. Suddenly Mr Murthy thought of something. 'I am sorry. You cannot be Krishna Bhagavan. You are an impostor.'

'What?' said Krishna.

Mr Murthy said, 'If you were really who you claim you are, you would have come dressed correctly.'

'What do you mean?'

'I mean, where is your golden crown with that peacock feather? And where are your dolphin-shaped earrings? And where is the silk cloth that you wear? And the sandalpaste marks you

anoint your face and body with? And
the garland of tulsi and champaka
flowers? Sorry, you cannot be Krishna
Bhagavan.'

'How do you know so much about
what I am supposed to wear?'

'I see your photo every day,
remember, when I serve you butter.
You do not look like the photo I see
every day. It is my job to look at
people's photos on their identity
cards and identify them. You don't
have an identity card. And you do
not look like the photo in my puja
room. So you cannot be Krishna
Bhagavan. So go away now, come
back with an identity card or I will
have you arrested.'

So it was that Krishna could not take his flight to Guwahati, the capital of Assam, to meet his old devotee, Latakumari, who had served him butter every morning for sixty-two years and was now ill and calling for him.

'What do I do now?' wondered Krishna.

'Go the way you usually go,' said Sesha, the giant golden snake with

seven heads, who was waiting in the airport parking lot in the shape of a giant yellow taxi. People around did not realize that the taxi was actually a giant snake with seven heads. They could not hear him speak either. Only Krishna could hear him. 'Call Garuda. He will take you to Guwahati,' Sesha advised.
'Where is he?' asked Krishna.

'Look up,' said Sesha. 'He is hovering overhead in the form of a helicopter. He can pick you up and take you to Lata-kumari in a minute. The plane will take at least three hours, maybe more, considering the delays while taking off and landing.'

'But I want to experience the plane. I

enjoy travelling with humans.'

'Stop behaving like a child, Krishna,'
said Sesha sternly. But he knew
Krishna would always be a child,
enjoying butter, enjoying the company
of people, enjoying planes and airports.

Krishna looked up towards the sky.

He saw a green and brown helicopter hovering above.

To most people, it appeared like a military helicopter. For Krishna it was Garuda. 'Maybe I should ask Garuda to take me to Guwahati.'

As soon as Krishna completed this sentence, the mighty eagle swooped down, picked him up, placed him on his back and flew at the speed of light over the clouds towards the east. Before Mr Murthy could blink, Garuda and Krishna were in the building where Lata-kumari lived. Garuda took the form of a motorbike and waited outside while Krishna entered the building.

The building had seven floors. Krishna

knew Lata-kumari lived with her son and daughter-in-law and two granddaughters in the fourth floor. He got into the lift of the building and went up four floors and entered Lata-kumari's house. 'He could have simply slipped through the walls,' Krishna could hear Garuda mumble in the building compound.

Krishna smiled. He had wanted to experience this thing the British call lift and the Americans call elevator. But he decided not to bother with the doorbell and to just pass through the walls, as if they did not exist. He entered Lata-kumari's room, unnoticed by other family members.

Lata-kumari was indeed very old. She

was over eighty years old. And she was tired all the time. She spent most of her day in her room, resting. When she was awake she prayed to her Krishna and if she had the strength, she told her grandchildren stories about Krishna.

'So you have finally come,' she said when Krishna came into her room. She lay in her bed, but she had taken a bath and was wearing her best sari as if she was waiting for a guest. Her wrinkled eyes sparkled as she saw this handsome visitor in her room. She was not at all surprised by the strange way he entered the room. In fact, she expected it.

'You recognize me?' said Krishna.

'Yes, you are Krishna Bhagavan. I had

this very strange dream. I saw you were
in an airport trying to catch a flight.
I saw that the security guard refused
to let you in because you did not have
your golden crown with the peacock
feather or your dolphin earrings, or
your silk dhoti or your garland. So
you went to the parking lot where you
met Sesha, who had taken the form of
a yellow taxi. He advised you to come

to me on your eagle, Garuda, who had taken the form of a helicopter. In that dream, you were dressed in a yellow T-shirt and faded blue jeans. So I recognized you,' said Lata-kumari.

'This identity card business can be quite irritating,' said Krishna.

'But it is useful. Imagine if you gods did not dress differently, how would we humans identify you?'

'What are you saying?'

'If you did not wear a crown with a peacock feather, how would anyone know you are Krishna?'

'That is true. I never thought of that.'

'I think it was Rishi Chavan who forced all gods to dress differently because of an ordeal the Ashwini-kumars made his wife, Sukanya, go through.'

'Is that so? Tell me the story. I love stories,' said Krishna, pulling a chair close to Lata-kumari's bed.

'You are Krishna Bhagavan. You know everything. You know all stories. Why do you want me to tell you a story?'

'Because,' said Krishna with a grin, 'hearing a story is more fun than knowing a story. Everyone tells stories differently. I am sure the way you will tell this story will be very different from how others say it. I want to enjoy both the story and the way Lata-kumari will narrate it.'

Lata-kumari was excited. Her eyes sparkled like a little girl's. Suddenly she did not feel old or weak. She felt like a storyteller. She would tell Krishna the story of Sukanya and the Ashwini-kumars.

Sukanya once saw two shiny bugs inside a termite hill. She shoved a twig into the termite hill to catch these bugs.

To her horror, she realized that they were not bugs, but the eyes of Rishi Chavan, who had been seated on the spot for a hundred years and meditating. He had sat so still that termites had built a hill over him. He had finished

meditating and had just opened his eyes,
when Sukanya, mistaking them for
shiny bugs, pierced them.

To atone for this crime, Sukanya's
father forced her to marry old Rishi
Chavan. 'Serve him well. He should
never miss his eyes that you destroyed,'

her father told her. Sukanya did
as told. She took care of Chavan,
attending to all his needs without a
word of protest, though in her heart
she felt miserable and wished things
had not turned out so badly.

One day the twin gods, the Ashwini-
kumars, paid her a visit. The Ashwini
twins are the morning and evening

stars that appear in the sky at dawn
and at dusk. Actually, they are not
stars. They do not twinkle. They
are planets. Not two planets; only
one, assumed to be two because they
can be seen next to the rising sun
in the morning and the setting
sun in the evening.

The Ashwini twins told Sukanya,
'Leave your old blind husband in the

forest and come with us to the city
of the gods.'

'No,' said Sukanya. 'My husband
needs me. I will not leave him.'

Pleased with this answer the Ashwini
twins offered to restore Chavan's
youth and eyesight. Sukanya could not

An Identity Card for Krishna

believe her luck. The two gods took the old rishi into a lake. 'Hold your breath,' said the two gods and all three of them plunged into the waters at the same time. A few minutes later, three youths emerged. All three were handsome. All three looked exactly alike.

One of them spoke to Sukanya, 'If you can identify who amongst us is Rishi Chavan, you can stay with him. Otherwise you have to leave him and

serve the Ashwini-kumars.' Sukanya
was for a moment perplexed. All three
looked the same. How would she
distinguish the gods from her husband?

But then she remembered something
her father had told her about the gods:
their feet never touch the earth!
She paid careful attention to the feet

of the three youths as they emerged
from the water and stepped on the
ground. Two of them floated on the

An Identity Card for Krishna

air. The soles of their feet were clean.
One of them stood firmly on the
ground. The soles of his feet were
dirty. Sukanya smiled and pointed to
the man with dirty feet, who she knew
for sure was her husband.

'You are a clever girl, Sukanya. And
a very good girl,' said the twin gods.
They blessed her and her husband,
and offered both of them a boon.

Sukanya said, 'You must always carry
a flag with your emblem, the horse,
on it. That way everyone will always
know who you are. You will not be
able to confuse others as you tried to
confuse me.'

Rishi Chavan said, 'Not just you two,

I want all gods to carry flags with their emblems so that humans can easily identify them.'

Since then all gods carry flags with

their emblems all the time. These are called 'dhvajas'.

Krishna was very happy to hear this story. 'Every year, in the city of Puri, Orissa, I go on a chariot ride with my brother, Balabhadra, and my sister, Subhadra. My chariot has my flag with the emblem of an eagle. It is called Garuda-dhvaja. My brother's chariot has his flag with the emblem of

a palm tree. It is called Tada-dhvaja.'

Lata-kumari added, 'Ganesha carries a flag with the emblem of a rat. And his brother, Kartikeya, carries a flag with the emblem of a rooster.' She then smiled and added, 'Even their father, Shiva, has a flag with his own emblem, a bull. It is called Vrishabha-dhvaja. And Kama, the god of love, has a flag with the emblem of a dolphin. It is called

Makara-dhvaja. Flags of gods are
their identity cards.'

'Gods need identity cards so that
humans are not confused. And
now humans need identify cards
so that security guards do not get
confused,' said Krishna with a smile,
remembering Mr Murthy who had
stopped him from entering the airport.

Lata-kumari said, 'During the
great Mahabharata war, when the
five Pandava brothers fought the
hundred Kaurava brothers, every
warrior carried a flag along with
his weapons. The five flags of the
Pandavas were very distinctive:
moon for the honest Yudhishthira,
lion for the mighty Bhima, monkey

for the archer Arjuna, deer for the handsome Nakula and swan for the wise Sahadeva. Their enemies, the

Kauravas, had flags with emblems too. I guess every warrior wanted everyone else on the battlefield to know who they were and who they were fighting.'

Krishna said, 'Every god had a specific identity card—the dhvaja. Humans

need a specific identity card too. I better get mine soon so that I can fly back to Mumbai on a plane.'

Outside Lata-kumari's window, Garuda and Sesha chuckled on hearing Krishna's plan.

Government of India

IDENTITY CARD

Name: Krishna Bhagawan

Address: Dwarka Nagari

ID NO: AFPTE481IRE—10

Shiva

Plays Dumb Charades

Can you speak without using your tongue? Yes, you can! Can you speak without using your mouth? Yes, you can! Can you speak without using words? Yes, you can! Try playing dumb charades, a game where you have to act out a word given to you by one friend so that other friends can guess what the word is. It is fun. That is why ABCDE played it.

Who are ABCDE? They are five kids who met for the first time when their parents gathered for a dinner party. A stands for Abhishek. B for Brinda. C for Chandrashekhar. D for Dilip. E for Eshwar. ABCDE. The party had been thrown by one of the parents. There ABCDE met each other, became great friends and played a game called dumb charades. And guess who joined the game? Shiva himself.

Shiva? Who is Shiva? He is a god. Not a small god but a big god. Not a Deva but Maha-Deva. That is why some say he should be called God, spelt with capitals, not god, without capitals.

How did Shiva come to play dumb charades with ABCDE? For that we

have to use our imagination and travel
back in time to that Sunday evening
of the dinner party. Instead of going
to the mall or watching a movie or just
staying home, three sets of parents,
and their five children, met in one
house to have fun.

The six adults sat in the front room drinking juices and talking about their childhood and their work, while food was being cooked in the kitchen. There were onion pakodas and potato chips on the table. The adults were busy talking, or eating, or drinking. They forgot that in the next room were the

five children — ABCDE — all alone, left
to themselves.

At first no one talked to anyone.
People are nervous when they meet
for the first time. They are afraid that
strangers will bite. ABCDE were no

different. Each one looked at the other suspiciously. But after some time, they all got so bored that they decided to introduce themselves to each other. With that a new friendship began.

They all sat down in front of the television to watch cartoons. It was fun for some time. Then they got bored.

So they played music and began
to dance. It was fun, but for some
time. Oh, so much boredom! But the
parents were busy talking and talking
and talking. Did they never get bored?

Shiva Plays Dumb Charades

Then Dilip had an idea. He suggested they use their hands to create shadow animals. It was fun for some time. Then someone suggested they play dumb charades. One person would whisper a

word in the ears of another, who would have to enact the word while the rest would guess what the word was. A, for example, said dog in the ears of B and B started behaving like a dog. But C and D and E thought that he was behaving like a crow, no a monkey, no a cow. They kept guessing and making mistakes and laughing and teasing and it was a whole lot of fun. So much fun that Shiva decided to join the gang.

'Can I play too?' a voice boomed. The children looked around and found in their room a big bull. On top of the bull sat a man who was wearing animal skins. He had ash on his face and his arms. He held a trident in his hand. There was a snake around his neck, and what looked like a moon on his

forehead. And a fountain rising up from the knot of hair on top of his head.

'You look like Shiva,' said the children.

'I *am* Shiva,' said Shiva. 'And I want to play. Guess what this is.' He turned

his palm down and stretched it in the
direction of the children.

What could it mean, the children
wondered. Was he pointing to the
floor? Was he asking for something?
The children gave up. Shiva smiled

and said, 'It means take this boon. If you go to the temple you will see the deity holding his or her hand in a particular way. These poses are called mudras. This pose, where the palm points downwards, indicates that the god or goddess is offering a boon. It is called varada mudra.'

ABCDE laughed.

Shiva said, 'I love playing games. I love presenting puzzles and expect my devotees to solve them. Here is one: see that moon on top of my head? Guess if it is the first day of the waxing moon or the last day of the waning moon.'

The children did not know the answer to this puzzle. 'Try, try,' said Shiva.

'Don't you look at the sky? Don't you study these things in geography class?' The children were embarrassed. 'Oh, don't be embarrassed. If you don't know, you don't know, it is okay,' said Shiva. 'Now observe carefully. Since the moon on my head is like a cup, it is the last day of the waning moon before it disappears from the sky on new moon night. If it had been like an overturned cup, it would be the waxing moon, the first day after the new moon night. When this moon appears in the sky before the new moon night people pray to me. It is called Shiv-ratri.'

ABCDE were surprised. They celebrated Shiv-ratri once a year. Now they learnt that there is a Shiv-ratri every month and the one that is celebrated by all is called Maha-Shiv-ratri which means 'the great night of Shiva'. The children wondered why Shiva is worshipped on that particular day. Shiva replied, 'So that the moon comes back again after the new moon.'

'But it always comes back even if you don't pray,' said the children.

So Shiva explained, 'My dear, the moon is not the moon you see in the sky. It is the moon that represents your moods. All of you feel happy sometimes and then bored, don't you?' The children nodded. 'Like when you were watching cartoons. You were happy for some time and then you became bored and sad. Then you were happy playing with shadows but you became sad again. You were all like the moon; your mood was waxing and waning, but it was way faster than the moon in the sky. People pray to me when they are upset and I try to cheer them up.'

'And the fountain on top of your head! What is that?' asked the children.

'That is Ganga,' said Shiva, 'the river. Once upon a time, this river flowed only in the sky. It still does. You can see it on a clear night. We call it the Milky Way. One day the gods told the river to flow on earth. The river agreed and jumped down. Had the river fallen on earth directly, it would have broken the foundations of the earth. So I stood between the sky and the earth, caught the river on my head and trapped it in my hair. Now she flows gently without hurting the earth.'

The children said, 'So you help the moon and you help the earth and you even help the river. You are a friend in need, so a real friend indeed!'

'Shall we continue with dumb charades or shall I give you another puzzle?'

'Dumb charade,' said A, B and C.

'Puzzle,' said D and E.

'Okay both,' said Shiva, enjoying himself thoroughly. He turned his

palm so that his fingers pointed upwards and stretched out his hand. 'What does this mean?' he asked.

The children thought and thought. 'It means stop!' said A. E said, 'It means a slap!'

'No,' said Shiva. 'It means calm down. Don't be afraid. This is abhaya mudra. Bhaya means fear. Abhaya means no fear.'

'Do not be afraid of what?' wondered the children.

'Look again,' said Shiva, striking a

pose. This pose, the children knew, was known as Nataraja, which means Lord of Dance.

The children realized that Shiva was pointing to something with his left hand. He was pointing to his left foot. The children noticed that the left foot was moving while the right foot was still and firmly placed on the ground. What was Shiva trying to communicate? This was no easy dumb charade.

Shiva said, 'This left foot is on the side of the body that has your heart. Your heart is always beating. The opposite side is

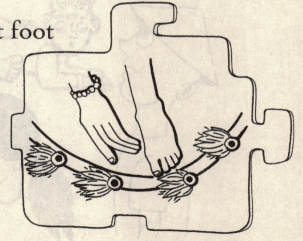

always still. Everything in this world, like your body, has two sides—one side that is always moving and one side that is still. Things that keep moving disturb us. I am telling you not to be afraid of movement.' Shiva paused for a bit and continued, 'Now look, both

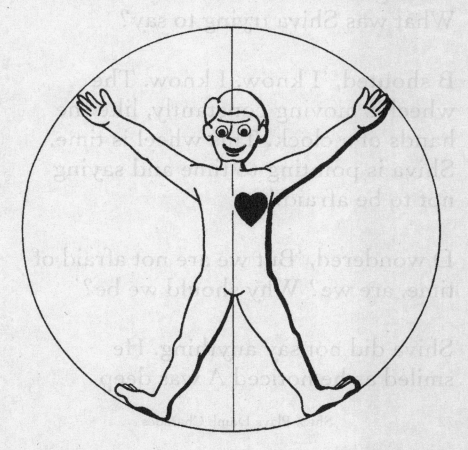

left hand and left feet are pointing to something else. What is it?'

The children noticed that the left foot and the left hand were pointing to a wheel. A big giant wheel that was moving round and round and round. What was Shiva trying to say?

B shouted, 'I know. I know. The wheel is moving constantly, like the hands of a clock. This wheel is time. Shiva is pointing to time and saying not to be afraid.'

D wondered, 'But we are not afraid of time, are we? Why should we be?'

Shiva did not say anything. He smiled as he noticed A was deep in thought. Shiva smiled encouragingly at A who shared his thoughts, 'I am afraid of time. When I am playing, which I love, time moves fast. When I am studying, which I hate, time moves slowly. Time hates me and so I hate time.'

D agreed with A, 'Every time I am having a good time, like watching movies, time moves fast. Every time I am having a bad time, like doing homework, time moves slow.'

B said, 'I think Shiva is telling us not to be afraid of time, whether it moves fast or slow. Time does not move fast or slow, but when our mind is happy it seems time is moving fast and when our mind is unhappy it's as though time is moving slowly. Our mind is changing the speed of time. That's it. That is what Shiva is telling us.'

Shiva smiled, 'You are clever children. I am very impressed.'

C noticed that Shiva was standing on top of what looked like a goblin. 'Who is that?' he asked.

Shiva said, 'That is the goblin of forgetfulness. He makes you forget. Do you remember what you ate day before yesterday for lunch?'

C could not remember. Nor could B

or A or E or D. 'No, we cannot,' they said in unison.

'When you are angry with your mother, you forget all the wonderful things she has done for you. And when you are happy with your father, you forget all the strict discipline he has imposed upon you. Right?' The children nodded.

Dileep remembered all the notes his mother stuck on the fridge to remind herself of tasks she had to do. Dileep realized that the demon of forgetfulness had struck his mother.

Shiva said, 'The demon of forgetfulness is the reason we get anxious and upset. When good things

happen, we forget all the bad things that happened in the past. And when bad things happen, we forget all the good things that happened in the past. We don't realize that good and bad things follow each other just like the waxing moon follows the waning moon. We forget that everything flows in and out like a river.'

B noticed that Shiva had two different earrings on his left and right ear. 'Don't you believe in matching your jewellery?' she asked.

Shiva replied, 'Oh, that is done deliberately. Another puzzle. Can you guess why?' B could not guess. So Shiva solved the puzzle. 'On the left side I am wearing a woman's earring. And on the

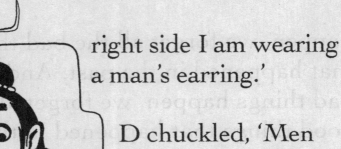

right side I am wearing a man's earring.'

D chuckled, 'Men don't wear earrings.'

E snapped, 'Of course they do. In olden days men too wore earrings. I have seen pictures of old statues where men wore earrings.'

B asked, 'Why do you wear male and female earrings?'

Shiva answered, 'To tell everyone that I love boys and girls equally.'

B smiled. She often noticed that girls are treated differently from boys.

Boys are allowed to go and play alone but girls are not. She was glad that Shiva treated boys and girls equally. She hugged Shiva.

'And why do you hold a drum in your hand?' asked E, realizing this was another puzzle.

'Have you seen this drum before?' asked Shiva. Yes, the children had seen the drum. They had seen it with men who train monkeys to do tricks. 'Yes, this is a rattle-drum to distract and control monkeys. Monkeys are very restless. Can you tell me which part of your body is the most restless?'

A said, 'Our feet.'

B said, 'Our hands.'

C said, 'Our eyes.'

D said, 'Our mouth.'

E said, 'I think it is our mind.'

Shiva said, 'E is right. Even when you sleep and your body is not moving, your mind is moving, dreaming of things to entertain or frighten you.' The children realized that was correct. 'The mind is just like a monkey—restless. That is why sometimes we are happy and sometimes we are sad. I am not just killing the demon of forgetfulness, I am also helping you so that you are not always restless and bored.'

The children remembered the image of three monkeys, one who shut his eyes, the second who shut his mouth and the third who shut his ears. E had heard his mother say, 'We have to train our mind like these three monkeys so that we do not see bad

things, or speak bad things or hear bad things.' Shiva's rattle-drum was meant to train the monkey mind.

'And fire? Why do you have fire in your other hand?' asked E.

'Because fire burns everything. Fire can burn all kinds of things and when a thing burns down, all that remains is ash. I hold fire in my hand to remind you that everything in this world comes to an end. Sunday will come to an end. The holidays will come to an end. Even this party will eventually come to an end. What will remain is memories. So use this time well and your memories will be happy ones.'

'And the snake? Why do you have a snake around your neck?' asked A. He could not believe that Shiva had so many puzzles on his body.

Shiva said, 'First answer this question: is it moving or is it still?' The children were puzzled. It is a living snake, of course it moves.

Then suddenly A realized something
and shouted, 'Hey, this snake is still.'

'Why do you say that?' asked B.

A replied, 'It is a cobra. It has a hood.
When does a cobra spread its hood?
When it is still. Not when it is
moving. This is a still snake. Is
it not? Am I right?'

Shiva looked pleased.
'You are a smart boy.
Many grown-ups have
not been able to answer
this question. I am so
still that even snakes
can climb on my body

and coil around my neck. They sit still because I am still and we both invite everyone around to sit still, not run around restless all the time.'

The children suddenly realized that all the gods and goddesses whose pictures they had seen were constantly playing dumb charades with their hands and feet, communicating different ideas and words. They have been playing dumb charades in temples for a very long time, expecting devotees to guess what they were saying. But while the gods continued to play, the devotees had stopped playing and so the gods were now left alone with their mudras that no one bothered to understand. 'I am sure our parents do not know how to play dumb charades with the gods,' they said.

The children spent the evening looking
at the image of the dancing Shiva and
trying to solve the puzzles. They thanked
Shiva for playing with them. Shiva
thanked them for solving his puzzles and

guessing his dumb charades. He then turned around and disappeared.

The parents of ABCDE stopped talking and gossiping when they realized there was no noise coming out of the children's room. Were they asleep? They peeped in and saw the children watching the image of the dancing Shiva intently. They wondered why. They could not understand. But the children did and they thanked Shiva for it.

Indra

Finds Happiness

Harsha sat on the terrace of his building. It was a warm summer day. There was a gentle breeze blowing from the east. In the sky, clouds were taking wonderful shapes. Some looked like horses and others like fish. But Harsha did not notice either the breeze or the clouds, because he was unhappy.

Why was Harsha unhappy? Harsha was unhappy because his parents were

fighting. His mother wanted to go out and watch a movie in a theatre while his father wanted to stay at home and watch a football match on television.

Harsha was unhappy because his sister had been on the mobile phone all day. Ever since she had passed out from school and joined college she found no time to play with him. But she always found time to

chat with her new college friends on her phone.

Harsha was unhappy because Ritwik Uncle was sitting at his desk groaning.

His stomach was upset and he had a headache. It had something to do with the party he had attended the previous night. No medicines worked. 'Leave me alone!' he had yelled when Harsha had entered his room.

Harsha wanted to play a video game. But his mother would not allow it. Harsha wanted to go out and play in his friend's house. But his father would not allow it.

Harsha wanted to eat an ice cream. 'Only after dinner,' his mother had said sternly.

Harsha had clearly many reasons to be unhappy. So he went to the terrace of his building and began feeling sorry for himself. 'I think I am the unhappiest person in the world,' he said.

'Oh, come on!' said a cloud in the sky. 'You are not the unhappiest person in the world. No one is as unhappy as Indra.'

Harsha looked up at the cloud. It looked like a huge cotton ball. 'Who is Indra?' he asked.

'He is the god of the sky, ruler of the

stars and the planets, the god who
makes rain fall on earth.'

'How can a god be unhappy?'
wondered Harsha.

'I will take you to his palace in the sky and you can ask him yourself,' said the cloud. That sounded like an interesting idea. Harsha jumped on the back of the talking cloud and it zoomed up like a rocket.

In less than a minute, Harsha found himself standing before Indra.

Indra was reclining on a grand throne that had many cushions on it. Above him was a rainbow. Below his feet were the stars.

'Welcome to paradise,' said Indra. 'I am Indra, ruler of the sky, the stars, the planets and the clouds. I am the unhappiest person in the world. And you must be Harsha, the boy who claims to

be the unhappiest person in the world.'

Harsha nodded his head.

'Do you know what your name means?' asked Indra.

'Yes,' said Harsha. 'It means the happy one.'

Indra sneered, 'Clearly not a good name for you.'

Harsha looked around. There was nothing in Indra's palace — no television, no music system, no computer, no books. It looked so empty. 'What do you do all day?' asked Harsha.

Indra said, 'I hunt clouds.'

Harsha looked at the cloud that had brought him before Indra. 'Oh, don't worry about me,' chuckled the cloud. 'He means he hunts grey clouds. I am a white cloud.'

'Yes,' said Indra. 'Grey clouds and black clouds are full of water. And they travel swiftly on the wind. I chase them on my elephant and hurl my thunderbolt at them. I break them open and cause rain to fall on earth.'

Harsha looked at Indra's elephant. He had white skin and three pairs of tusks, six in all. His name was Airavata. 'I was born in the ocean of milk,' said Airavata, explaining his white complexion.

'Grey clouds are not easy to find. They

hide under the sea but come out a few
times a year to feed on sunlight. That is
when Indra hunts them down. That is
when it rains on earth. Without Indra,
the earth would be dry
and barren,' said
the cloud. 'There
would be no fields
or orchards
or forests, just
sandy desert
everywhere.'

'Because of
my services, I
have been given
many gifts,' said
Indra. 'Come,
let me show
them to you.'

Indra Finds Happiness

There was a giant tree in Indra's garden. 'That is Kalpataru,' said Indra. 'Sit under it and wish for what you want.'

Harsha sat under the tree and wished for a chocolate. Almost immediately, his favourite chocolate appeared in his hand.

Harsha then wished for a report card that showed he had scored A grades in every subject. He had never been able to achieve that. Instantly, a piece of paper floated into his hand. It was the school report card and it showed he had scored an A in every subject including Math and English.

Harsha then wished for more

chocolates and a football and a new school bag. All that he wished for appeared before him as soon as he made his wish. 'This tree is a wish-fulfilling tree, is it not?' he asked. Indra nodded his head.

The cloud then showed Harsha a jewel. 'This is the Chintamani,' said the cloud. 'Like Kalpataru, it has the power to fulfil any dream of yours.'

'I dream of more chocolates and another football,'

said Harsha. Before he had completed
this sentence, six more chocolates and
a shiny new football streamed out of
the Chintamani. 'So all Indra has to do
is wish or dream
and he will get
what he wants?'
Harsha asked.

'Yes,' said the
cloud.

'Why then is
he unhappy?'
wondered Harsha.

'Wait, there
is more,' said
Airavata, the
elephant. 'See,

over there is Akshaya Patra, the pot that overflows with gold. Indra is richer than all the rich men on earth put together.'

'Why then is he unhappy? Maybe he is ill, like Ritwik Uncle?'

'He can never fall ill,' said Airavata. 'Indra has in his possession a jar containing Amrita.'

'What is Amrita?'

'It is a magic potion. He who drinks it never falls ill and never grows old. Even weapons cannot hurt him.'

'How lucky!' exclaimed Harsha. 'So Indra never has to go to the doctor's clinic. No injection, no medicines, no medical tests, no hospital. I would love to take a sip of Amrita.'

'No, no,' said Indra, rushing to Harsha's side. 'Amrita is only for me. I churned it out with great difficulty from the ocean of milk.'

'Churned an ocean! How did you do that?'

'I tell you it was not easy,' said Indra. 'We needed a mountain

as the spindle. We needed a turtle to keep the mountain from sinking to the bottom of the ocean. And for the churning rope we used a giant serpent. It took a hundred years to get a single drop of Amrita.'

'You have everything, Indra,' said Harsha. 'You have a tree that fulfils every wish and a gem that turns any dream into reality and a pot that is overflowing with gold and Amrita that keeps you healthy and young all the time. Why then are you unhappy?'

'First you tell me why you are unhappy,' said Indra.

Harsha replied, 'I am unhappy because my parents are fighting, my sister does not want to play with me and Ritwik Uncle wants me to leave him alone. I am unhappy because my mother will not let me play video games, my father will not let me go out of the house and I am not allowed to eat ice cream until after dinner.'

'My problem is bigger than your problem,' said Indra. 'I am afraid that all that I have will go away. One day, the Kalpataru will be cut down and the Chintamani will be stolen or I may lose the Akshaya Patra or Amrita. What will happen to me then?'

'Who will take them away from you?'

'A king, maybe.'

'How can a king take away what you have?' asked Harsha.

'A king can perform a ritual called a yagna. The yagna gives him powers. Armed with these powers he follows his royal horse and is able to conquer all the lands his horse travels into. I am afraid that one day such a king will have enough powers to conquer the sky and drive me away.'

'What a terrible thought! How will

you stop this from happening?'
wondered Harsha, concerned.

'Every time I see a king perform a
yagna, I steal the king's horse,' said
Indra slyly. A god who
steals! Harsha did
not like that.

Airavata
told Harsha
the story of
King Sagara
whose horse
Indra had
stolen.

Sagara ordered
his sons to find
the horse.

Indra Finds Happiness

The sons searched every corner of earth but could not find the horse. 'You have searched above the earth,' said Sagara to his sons, 'but have you searched below?'

Sagara's sons immediately began

digging the earth in search of the horse. They dug so much earth that a giant hole appeared in the ground. The horse was never found but when the rains came, the hole dug by Sagara's sons was filled with water. It is what we now call the sea. That is why the sea is called Sagara.

Harsha liked this story. Indra then continued sharing his problems. 'I am also afraid of sages who meditate.'

'Why?' asked Harsha.

'Because I fear they will discover some magic that will make it possible for them to kick me out of the skies. Then they will ride Airavata and hunt rain-clouds instead of me. They will become masters of my tree and my gem and my pot, and of Amrita too.'

'So what do you do when you find a sage meditating?'

'I send an apsara to dance and sing in front them. Apsaras are experts in singing and dancing. Their song and dance distracts the sages at first. Later they enjoy the song and dance

Indra Finds Happiness

so much that they forget all about meditation.'

'This apsara sounds like my television,' said Harsha.

Airavata laughed.
So did the cloud.

'Yes, yes,' said Indra. 'Apsaras are just like television. They don't let the sages meditate and the television does not let you study. You are a clever boy, Harsha.'

'If I give up television, maybe I can become a sage and discover a way to throw you out.'

'Please don't say that,' pleaded Indra. 'I would rather you watch television and do not study. Then you can become neither a sage nor a king.'

Harsha realized Indra had a fantastic imagination. The god kept imagining problems and threats all day. This kept him unhappy all the time.

Airavata then told Harsha the story of a sage called Kandu. An apsara called Marisha danced before him so beautifully that he lost all sense of time. For him a hundred nights became equal to a single night—such

Indra Finds Happiness

was the power of the apsara's song and dance. Kandu begged the apsara to stay with him forever. 'I will,' said Marisha. 'But promise me you will never spy on me in the evening when the sun is setting.'

Kandu promised he would never do so. But one day, after many happy years with Marisha, he could not resist spying on her in the evening. He followed her to a lake and there she turned into a swan as soon as the sun set.

In this form, she swam in the water until the sky became dark. Then she turned back into a woman. Marisha sensed that her husband had spied on her. She looked at Kandu and said, 'Because you broke your promise and

because you saw me in the form of
a swan, I will not stay with you any
more. I will go back to Indra.' Marisha
rose up to the sky. Kandu regretted his
curiosity and spent the rest of his life
thinking of her.

'What a sad story,' said Harsha.

Indra did not care for Kandu or the other sages who had been distracted by the song and dance of the apsaras. 'You know,' Indra confided, 'I can handle an ambitious king or a sincere sage but I cannot handle demons. When they attack me, I feel helpless. I have to take the help of other gods.'

Airavata told Harsha that once there was a demon called Taraka. Only a baby could kill him. Naturally, Indra could not defeat him in battle. Indra ran to Shiva and begged Shiva to give him his infant son, Kartikeya, who was barely six days old. Kartikeya rose from his cradle, picked up a spear, challenged Taraka to a fight and

defeated him in battle.

'A baby killed a demon!'

'Yes,' said Airavata. 'That baby is now Indra's commander. He protects Indra's city from demons.'

'Why then does Indra worry so much?' wondered Harsha.

'I cannot help it,' moaned Indra. 'Every time I try to relax, my mind is filled with images of kings and

sages and demons who want to take what I have. Oh, I must be the most miserable god in the world.'

'You are certainly more miserable than me,' said Harsha.

Indra asked Harsha, 'So what do you do when you feel sad?'

Harsha answered, 'I play video games.' 'Let's play video games,' said Indra.

Kalpataru instantly produced a video game for Indra. Harsha showed Indra how to play. Indra enjoyed it immensely. 'It's like fighting without fighting.'

The two of them played for several hours (remember, several hours in Indra's paradise is not more than a few seconds on earth). Indra won some games. Harsha won many more. It felt good to defeat a god in a game. But then Indra said, 'I am bored.'

'You should get a mobile phone,' said Harsha. 'Then you can talk to all your friends whenever you want. You can send text messages, jokes.'

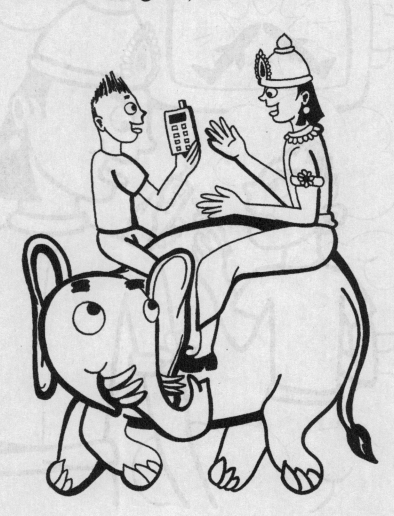

'Would it not be easier to go and simply meet them?' said Indra, climbing on the back of Airavata and pulling Harsha up to sit beside him. 'Yes, but sometimes people are far away and you want to talk to them. Then you need a mobile phone. Humans cannot fly, you know.'

'I don't think I like mobile phones. People pay more attention to mobile phones than to people in front of them. I find that very rude.'

Harsha looked at Indra's unhappy face. 'Let us eat ice cream. That should cheer you up. It always cheers me up.'

Chintamani brought forth ice cream. Indra chose butterscotch while Harsha

took dark chocolate while the cloud
ate plain old vanilla.

'I think if I had the cow Kamadhenu
I would be truly happy,' said Indra
suddenly.

'What is Kamadhenu?' asked Harsha.

'It is a cow that belongs to a sage
called Vasishtha. It is a cow that can
fulfil every wish.'

'Why do you want that?' asked
Harsha. 'You already have a tree that
fulfils all your wishes and a jewel that
turns all your dreams into reality.'

'Yes, but Vasishtha has this cow. What
if his wishes destroy my wishes? What

if Kamadhenu is more powerful than
Kalpataru and Chintamani? What will
happen then?'

'You worry so much. More than my
father and Ritwik Uncle and my sister.
My mother says that if you worry so
much you will get boils on the skin

and your head will fall off and your stomach will be full of gas.'

'Only one way to solve this. I must steal Kamadhenu from Vasishtha. Come with me. You can enter the sage's house and bring the cow out so that I can bring it to my palace. The sage will recognize me, but not you.'

'I will not steal,' said Harsha firmly.

'You are a coward,' said Indra. 'Be brave. Fetch the cow for me.'

Harsha refused to change his mind. 'Fine,' said Indra. 'I will fetch the cow myself.'

Indra entered Vasishtha's ashram

and caught hold of Kamadhenu
and began dragging her out.
'Master, master,' shouted the cow,
'Indra is trying to take me away
from you.'

Vasishtha heard his cow cry and
ran to her rescue.

He boxed Indra under the ears.
Indra fell to the ground with a thud.
'How dare you try to take what is not
yours? You should behave more like
a king and a god, and less like a thief,'
Vasishtha scolded Indra, who lowered
his head in shame.

'I just want to be happy,' said Indra.

'So do I,' said Harsha.

'Is that all?' said Vasishtha with a smile. 'That is easy.'

'Please tell us,' said Indra and Harsha in unison.

Vasishtha said, 'You can be happy if you are satisfied with what you have.

If you wish for more than what you have, you will always be unhappy.'

'That's it?' said Indra. 'It cannot be that simple.'

'It is that simple,' said the sage. 'You can have a hundred Kalpatarus and a hundred Chintamanis and a hundred Akshaya Patras and all the Amrita in the world, but that will not make you happy unless you are satisfied with them. Happiness depends on you, not on what you possess. Just sit down in one place, shut your eyes, and think about what I said. It is the truth, the greatest truth.'

Indra went back to his paradise, sat on his throne and thought about what

Vasishtha had said: 'You can be happy if you are satisfied with what you have. If you wish for more than what you have, you will always be unhappy.' It made no sense to Indra. He kept thinking about Vasishtha's cow and felt more miserable than before.

The cloud brought Harsha back to his house. His parents were still fighting, his sister was still on the mobile phone and Ritwik Uncle was still feeling unwell.

Harsha went to his room and sat down and thought about what Vasishtha had said: 'You can be happy if you are satisfied with what you have. If you wish for more than what you have, you will always be unhappy.' It made sense.

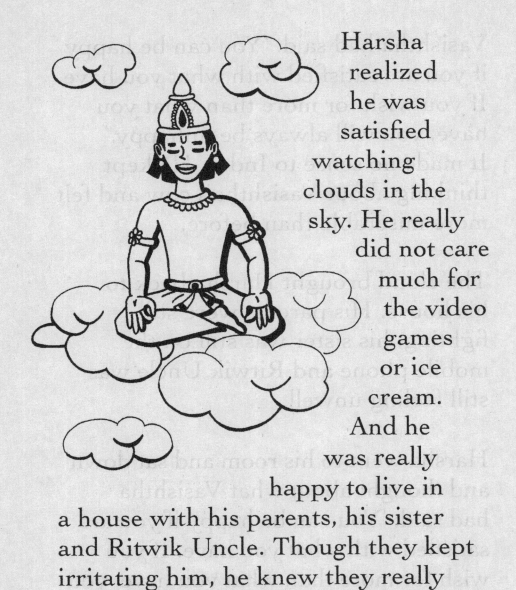

Harsha realized he was satisfied watching clouds in the sky. He really did not care much for the video games or ice cream. And he was really happy to live in a house with his parents, his sister and Ritwik Uncle. Though they kept irritating him, he knew they really cared for him. Harsha realized he did not want Indra's tree or his gem or his pot or even Amrita, even though they were truly wonderful. He did not

even want Vasishtha's cow. He was
satisfied with the things around him.
He was happier than Indra, god of the
sky. He smiled.

Saraswati's

Secret River

On Tuesday morning, Mrs Sivakami, principal of Madame Mira High School, in the town of Mirapur, found Saraswati walking down the school corridor, her pet goose behind her, peeping into classrooms. Yes, it was Saraswati, the goddess of learning. She looked just like the image kept at the school entrance. She wore a white sari, had a book and a pen in one hand, and a stringed musical instrument in another. Was it a veena or a sitar or a tanpura? Mrs Sivakami was not curious to know. She was just too surprised and much pleased to have a goddess as a visitor to her school.

Mrs Sivakami had spent ten years teaching English, History and Geography at the school. Every year she taught eighty students. This means in ten years she had taught the three subjects to eight hundred students. No, eight hundred and ten students! Last year and the year before last, she had eighty-five students in her class, accounting for the ten extra students. She was sure that some day somebody would appreciate her for teaching so many subjects to so many students. Could

it be that the goddess was looking for her? Could it be the goddess had come down to appreciate her? No harm hoping, she told herself, as she walked towards the goddess.

'Can I help you?' she asked Saraswati in an extremely polite voice.

Instead of replying, the goddess caught the teacher's ear. 'Do you realize that the river will stop flowing in your school very shortly?' The goddess sounded rather agitated.

'River? There is no river in our school,' said a very startled Mrs Sivakami. She was not used to having her ear held so. 'There is a pond, near the back gate. But no river, I am sure of it. What is

the name of this river which you say will dry up?'

'River Saraswati, of course,' replied the goddess in a calm melodious voice.

'Is that not your name?' asked Mrs Sivakami.

'It is my name. It is also the name of the river that was named after me. Surely you have heard of it? Don't you teach History and Geography?'

'Yes, but I have not heard of such a river anywhere near our school.' Mrs Sivakami was afraid that the goddess was here to punish her. 'Oh, please don't twist my ears. I will find the river, I promise you,' she pleaded in a voice that quivered. She felt her knees wobble. Is that how her students felt when she shouted at them, she wondered. But the goddess was not shouting. She was smiling and sounding very sweet, she noticed.

Why then were her knees shaking?

'Twist your ears? Why would I do that?' asked Saraswati, sounding rather surprised.

'Er . . . you are holding my ear,' Mrs Sivakami pointed out with a sheepish grin.

'Oh that.' The goddess laughed, releasing Mrs Sivakami's ear. 'I thought I saw wax in your ear. Just checking.'

'Ugh,' said Mrs Sivakami, feeling rather offended. 'I clean my ears every Sunday with cotton buds. There cannot be any wax in my ears.'

'Please don't be upset. I like ears to

be clean. How else will you listen to what I have to say?' said Saraswati once again peeping into the principal's ear, just to make sure. 'Since you have never heard of River Saraswati, or seen it flowing in your school, you clearly would not notice if it was dying, now would you?'

Mrs Sivakami did not know how to respond. She wondered what was the proper way to address the goddess. Should she call her Goddess or Madam or Saraswati-ji or simply Saraswati? Would the goddess mind? No one teaches these things at school, or at home. No one prepares you with a situation where you are face-to-face with a goddess. Teachers are as clueless as students.

Mrs Sivakami ventured cautiously, 'Madam-ji, could it be you are referring to the River Saraswati mentioned in the Vedas?' The Vedas are ancient books of knowledge, containing hymns composed over 4,000 years ago.

'Yes, so you know about it.' The goddess felt relieved.

'I believe that river dried up.'

'Oh it still flows—secretly,' said Saraswati's goose flapping her wings. Her name was Hansa.

'Where?' exclaimed Mrs Sivakami. 'In my school? Is this a joke?'

'Not quite,' said the goddess. 'Would you like to see the river when it flowed on earth?'

'Oh yes, I would. I heard it was a mighty river before it disappeared. Some say it flows underground and is the third river that joins the rivers Ganga and Yamuna at Prayag Sangam near the city of Allahabad. See, I know my history, and my geography,' Mrs Sivakami proclaimed smugly.

Saraswati picked up Mrs Sivakami by her waist and placed her on Hansa's back. She then sat on the goose and off they went to see the River Saraswati.

'Have you flown on a goose before?' asked Hansa.

'No. I do not think any human can. Hey, I always thought that Saraswati rides a swan.'

'Artists prefer drawing a swan than a goose,' said Hansa, sounding a little bitter. 'A swan is much more elegant than a goose, you see.'

'Actually, I usually ride a male goose or gander,' explained Saraswati. 'But today Hansa insisted on coming along with me. I like Hansa. She is no ordinary bird. Give her a mixture of milk and water, and she can separate the milk and the water. She reminds all students that to be good at studies they must separate that which is more important, indicated by milk, from that which is less important, indicated by water.'

'Wow,' said Mrs Sivakami. That was a lovely thought.

As Hansa glided through the clouds, Mrs Sivakami realized that they were also travelling back in time. The goddess was taking her to a distant place several thousand years in the past. Finally, from above the clouds, Mrs Sivakami saw a silver river flowing in a valley between vast golden mountains. Along both banks of the river were lush green forests dotted with tiny houses. 'That was the River Saraswati. Those are the schools on the banks of the river,' said Hansa. 'And look, there are the students studying under trees.'

Saraswati told Mrs Sivakami

something the teacher could not
believe. 'These students can leave these
schools any time they wish. No one is
forcing them to study. They are there
because they really want to learn.'

'Do you know what is the most

curious thing about your school, Mrs Sivakami?' asked Hansa.

'Tell me please.'

'When the school bell rings at the end of the day, all the students in your school scream joyfully.'

'I tell them to be quiet,' Mrs Sivakami defended herself. 'But these kids do not listen.'

'Oh, Mrs Sivakami, have you not wondered why they are so happy when the final school bell rings? Clearly they do not enjoy coming to school. They feel trapped and shout in joy to celebrate their release.'

'What nonsense!'

'It is true,' said Hansa. 'Please see these schools. The students enjoy studying here because the teacher does not force them to learn anything. The teacher simply makes sure that the student wants to learn new things. Once a student is curious, he will learn

on his own. No need of breathing down his or her neck.'

Saraswati pointed out some students who were looking at trees. 'Those students are interested in trees and are observing trees carefully to find out how the seed germinates, how the flower turns into fruit, how the colour of leaves change with the seasons. They end up studying Botany.'

Saraswati pointed out students who were in the kitchen. 'Those students are wondering what is the difference between food that is boiled and steamed and roasted and fried. So they are sitting with the cook and observing what these different processes do to food. They will end up learning about Chemistry and Physics, even some Biology, while learning how to cook.'

'And those kids,' said Hansa, 'they are in the stables watching the cow give birth to a calf. Yesterday, they spent all day in the forest watching the deer graze and the tiger hunt. They are interested in Zoology.'

'In my school we have books and videos on Botany and Zoology and

Chemistry and Physics in the library.
But no one reads the books or watches
those videos,' said Mrs Sivakami
sounding very depressed.

'That is because your students are
not curious. They are studying only
because they want to pass the exams,
not because they want to learn,' said
the goddess.

'Are my students bad?' asked Mrs Sivakami with a frown on her face.

'No, no,' said Saraswati hugging her. 'No student is bad. But if they do not learn, who loses?'

'They do.'

'So they should feel bad about not going to your library and not reading the books and not watching the videos. Not you.'

'But I am their teacher.'

'Teachers can teach only when students want to learn. No one can help a student who does not want to learn just as no one can wake up a boy

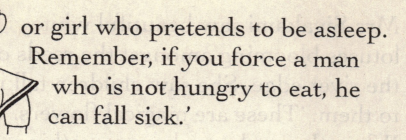

or girl who pretends to be asleep. Remember, if you force a man who is not hungry to eat, he can fall sick.'

These were very wise words, Mrs Sivakami realized. She reflected on these words for a long time, until Hansa said, 'Look at the lotuses.'

Mrs Sivakami saw beautiful white lotuses blooming amongst the reeds on the river edge. She saw children talking to them. 'These are magical flowers. When the students share something that they have genuinely learnt, the lotus blooms. When the students lie and simply rattle out what they have memorized, the lotus withers.'

Mrs Sivakami gasped. 'Never heard of such lotuses. Is that why the river is called Saraswati, after you, the goddess of learning?' Saraswati grinned and Hansa swooped down towards the students. The students waved out to the goddess. She waved back.

Mrs Sivakami noticed a group of students watching a crow. She heard

the students say, 'A good student must
be like a crow. Just as a crow bathes
quickly so must a student not waste
time on bathing for long periods of
time so that there is more time for
observation and study.'

She then saw another group of students watching a dog. She heard the students say, 'A good student must be like a dog. Even when asleep, a dog's ears are alert to surrounding sounds. So must a student be, eager to learn, not lost in deep slumber.'

She saw another group of students watching a heron. She heard the students say, 'A good student must be like a heron. Look how patiently it stands on one foot waiting for its meal. And how every time it strikes the water, it comes up with a fish between

its beaks. This bird teaches us patience and concentration.'

'Nature teaches us so much. I feel a good student is like a river, never looking back, always forward, moving in the direction of knowledge,' said Mrs Sivakami, feeling inspired by the students on the banks of the River Saraswati. 'I love this place. It is a pity that this river disappeared.'

'Don't you want to know why?' asked Hansa.

'I assume it was because of some natural disaster, like an earthquake.'

'Maybe something else happened,' said Saraswati, sounding mysterious.

Mrs Sivakami saw the scene change
before her eyes. The lotus flowers
started to wither. The river shrunk in
size. The teacher's head was replaced
by that of a parrot. The students' heads
were also replaced by that of parrots.

Saraswati's Secret River

'Why do they have parrot heads?' Mrs Sivakami wondered aloud.

'Think. Figure it out yourself,' said Saraswati smiling encouragingly.

'Parrots can remember and repeat words and speak like human beings. But they do not understand what they are saying. As far as they are concerned, these are only sounds that humans have taught them to say.'

'Go on,' said Saraswati.

'Aha! These students and their teacher do not know what they are talking about. They are simply memorizing lessons without understanding them.'

'Yes,' said the goddess. 'If you remember something, you can rattle it out without an error to another student. This will help information pass from one person to another. That is good. However, if you only memorize and do not understand, that is bad. And sad.'

Hansa then told the never-before-told story of the river that once flowed on earth. The schools on either side of Saraswati forgot the value of curiosity and learning. They simply memorized what was transmitted by other students and teachers and schools. Gradually the white lotuses on the river's edge, tired of waiting for genuine students, withered away and became extinct. Even the river slowly

began to
shrink in
size. Before
long, it was
nothing
more than a
tiny stream.
It finally
slipped out
of earth.
People
forgot all
about the
river, the
lotuses and
the schools on the riverbanks.

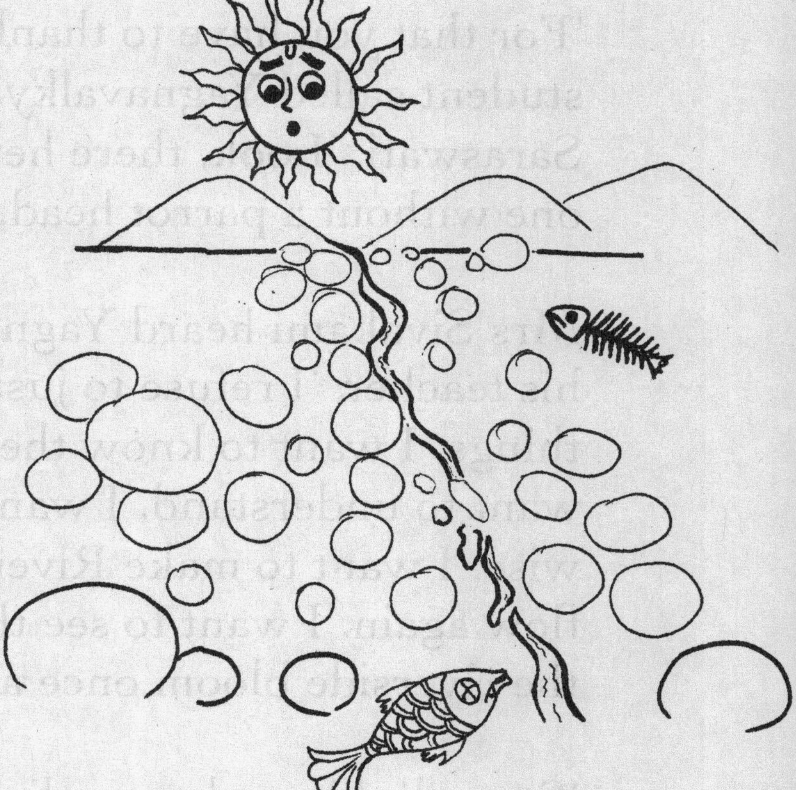

'What a sad story!' said Mrs Sivakami.
'But you said River Saraswati flowed
in my school. How did it reappear?'

'For that you have to thank a young student called Yagnavalkya,' said Saraswati. 'Look, there he is, the only one without a parrot head.'

Mrs Sivakami heard Yagnavalkya tell his teacher, 'I refuse to just memorize things. I want to know the meaning. I want to understand. I want to become wise. I want to make River Saraswati flow again. I want to see the lotuses on the riverside bloom once again.'

'Stop all this understanding and wisdom nonsense. Just memorize. If you rattle out what you remember, everyone will assume you are clever and everyone will respect you,' said his teacher. Yagnavalkya refused. 'You stubborn boy. If you don't like

remembering things then vomit out all
that I have taught you.'

'Fine,' said Yagnavalkya. He then put
his fingers in his mouth, tickled the
back of his throat until he belched and

vomited out all the hymns and chants
his teacher had told him to remember.
The sight disgusted Mrs Sivakami.

Then Yagnavalkya realized the sun
sees everything. So he deduced that
the sun knows everything. 'Will you be
my teacher?' he asked the sun.

'Yes,' said the sun. 'But only if you can catch me.'

So Yagnavalkya ran to the east to catch the rising sun. But the sun, after rising, moved west. So Yagnavalkya chased the sun to the west. But in the west, the sun set and Yagnavalkya did not know where to find the sun.

The next day he chased the sun again from the east to the west only to find the sun slipping away down the horizon in the west. 'Oh, my teacher is always running. I will never catch up with it. What do I do?'

'Maybe you should simply stop running,' said the sun with a smile. 'Just sit and wait. Every morning I

will appear
in the
east, rise
up and
move
across
the
sky
and then
slip into the
west. Just
sit in one
place and pay
attention to all
that I throw light
on. The more attention you pay, the
more you will want to know.'

'And who will give me the answers?'
asked Yagnavalkya.

'You will find out yourself. That is the best way to get answers. Teachers can only help you discover. But ultimately the responsibility is on you, the student. Saraswati will never chase you, you must chase Saraswati,' said the sun.

Yagnavalkya did as told. He sat down in one place and observed everything

that the sun shed its light on. And the
more he observed, the more he thought
about things and the more he learnt
and understood.

'What about at night, when the
sun does not shine in the sky?' he
wondered.

So the sun took the form of a horse
called Hayagriva and came to him
at night and spent the night talking
to him. Yagnavalkya shared with
the horse what he had observed and
learnt during the day. They argued
and debated. And Yagnavalkya was
able to improve his understanding
of things. He realized over time that
what one knows is but a drop of water
while what one does not know is an

ocean. Only if one has a great thirst
for knowledge will one get to know all
that there is to know in the world.

Hayagriva was very happy with
Yagnavalkya's curiosity and sincerity
and passion for learning. 'Ask a boon,'
said Hayagriva.

'I want River Saraswati to flow once again,' said Yagnavalkya.

'So be it,' said Hayagriva. 'The River Saraswati will flow once again.'

'Where?' Mrs Sivakami could not contain her curiosity. 'In my school?'

'Look, the secret river has finally started to flow in her,' said Hansa, pointing her wings at Mrs Sivakami.

'What?! I don't understand. Please explain,' said Mrs Sivakami.

Hansa spread out her wings dramatically and said, 'Saraswati now flows not outside the school but inside the student. Every time you are curious—as you are now—every time you want to know the answer to a question or a solution to a problem, the river Saraswati starts to flow, not on earth, but in your mind. That is the secret river, the invisible river—Saraswati!'

'Oh,' said Mrs Sivakami, her eyes widening. It dawned on her why the

goddess kept saying that the river Saraswati had stopped flowing in her school. Her students were no longer curious. In fact, when students showed even the slightest signs of curiosity, they were discouraged by her.

If they wanted to visit the library to read science magazines, she would

stop them saying, 'You have a History
test tomorrow. Why are you reading
Science when you should be reading
History?' Or if they wanted to watch
a video on space exploration, she
would stop them saying, 'But is that
in your syllabus?'

'I am turning the students into parrots.
I am causing River Saraswati to dry up!

I am no different from Yagnavalkya's teacher,' Mrs Sivakami wailed.

Saraswati comforted her. 'Don't worry. If you can find at least one student who is genuinely curious then it means River Saraswati still flows in your school.'

Mrs Sivakami remembered Rohit.

Rohit studied in the sixth standard in division D. He was always flipping through encyclopedias in the library or searching for stuff on the Internet. He wanted to know why leaves are green

and why a mango fruit has a seed but
a banana does not. He wanted to know
the name of Mahatma Gandhi's father
and Chanakya's mother. He spent
hours looking at the map trying to
locate countries and their capital cities.
The funny thing is that his parents saw
this as a problem! They came to the
school and complained, 'He never does
his homework or studies for exams. He

is only asking questions and seeking answers on various topics that are not part of his school syllabus. What should we do?'

Mrs Sivakami laughed. She had thought Rohit was a problem when in

fact he was ensuring that Saraswati, the river, was flowing in the school.

'Take me back home,' she requested Hansa. 'I want to thank Rohit. I also want to make sure that Saraswati's secret river flows in all my students.'

'It will be our pleasure,' said the goddess of learning plucking the strings of her musical instrument with great satisfaction.

Kama
vs
Yama

You would not recognize him if you saw him. But perhaps, you would not see him at all. Most people would not. Long ago, he had been cursed: 'You shall lose your body and become invisible.'

But on one sunny day, he became visible to a little girl called Jayshree. Of course, when Jayshree saw him she did not recognize him. It had been a long time since anyone had seen him.

Jayshree was a strange little girl. She loved doing homework! As soon as she got home from school, she would wash her face and hands and feet, change her clothes, have her lunch and then sit down to do her homework. She would make a list of things to do, then do them, then revise what she had done, revise them again, and finally pack her bags for the next day.

When she slept, she dreamt about what homework she would be given the following day.

'Come, watch TV with us,' her father would say.

And Jayshree would reply, 'No, Daddy. I have homework to do.'

'Go out and play,' her mother would say.

And Jayshree would reply (you guessed it), 'No, Mummy, I have homework to do.'

But on that sunny day, Jayshree had this mysterious desire not to do

homework. She just wanted to lie down on her bed, watch television and eat potato chips. Never ever had Jayshree experienced such a desire! She wanted to put her pen down, shut her notebooks, munch on chips and watch some silly cartoon. The idea made her smile.

Should I do this or should I do that? Homework or chips? As she was thinking, she heard a commotion in the garden. It was on the far side, so she could not see who it was despite stretching her neck through her window. When the commotion continued, she went out to check who it was.

'Who is there?' Jayshree shouted.

'It is me, Kama,' came a sweet voice.

Kama? Who Kama? Jayshree stepped out and saw a very handsome man in the garden. He was wearing bright robes that changed colour every time he moved. He was admiring the lotus buds in the lotus pond in the middle of the garden. 'Excuse me, who are you?'

'You can see me? You can really see me? I don't believe it! This must be my lucky day!' said the man in the colourful robe.

Jayshree saw that he held a cane of sugar in his hand. It was a tall purple staff with green leaves on the top. It waved with the wind. Around it were a few honey bees. Strange, Jayshree thought. Who was this man?

'Of course I can see you. Why should I not?' asked Jayshree.

'Because I have been cursed that I shall lose my body and stay invisible. For thousands of years I have wandered this world invisible with my sugar cane bow. And now you can see

Kama vs Yama

me. This is a miracle. You must be a special child. What is your name?'

'Jayshree,' said Jayshree, wondering if she should call her mother. Kama seemed harmless and was extremely charming but he was a stranger nevertheless. And what was he doing in their garden with a shaft of sugar cane?

'You can call your mother but she will not see

me,' said Kama. 'No one can. I am surprised that you can see me.'

'You can read my thoughts!' Jayshree was alarmed and a little scared.

'I am a god, silly girl. Don't they teach you anything in school? Look at my feet; they don't touch the ground. And look carefully, I don't blink. And I don't sweat. What is the use of all that homework that you so love to do?' Jayshree did not know how to react. 'Oh, don't think so much, girl. Let us play. It has been ages since a human saw me. It feels good. Let us celebrate this moment. Let us play. Or would you rather watch television and eat chips? I love chips too.'

Suddenly hundreds of butterflies
entered the garden. They danced
around Kama's head. Kama spread
out his hand and walked around
the garden. And in every direction

he went, tender shoots of grass
burst forth from the ground and
trees exploded to release flowers of
all colours. Every flower released
the sweetest of perfumes in the air.
Golden nectar enclosed by their petals
glittered in the sunlight. Dozens
of parrots descended from the sky.
They had bright red beaks and bright
green feathers. They sat on Kama's
shoulders and flapped their wings as
if to welcome an old friend.

Jayshree was overwhelmed by the
heady scent and the bright colours
around her. She forgot all about her
homework!

'That is what this idiot does. Makes
you forget homework and all the

important things you are supposed to do,' boomed a voice.

Jayshree turned and saw a black buffalo right behind her, chewing the grass thoughtfully and looking at her as if she was a criminal. Jayshree felt guilty and shameful. She did not know why.

On top of this buffalo was a stern looking man. He wore dull grey robes that were crumpled and his lips looked as if they had never curved to smile and he had a big thick and very long moustache.

In his hand he held a diary. 'I can see,' said the man, referring to his diary, 'that you have just finished your English homework. There is still Math

Kama vs Yama

and Science waiting to be done. And
you have to cover your Geography
book with brown paper. The old cover
is damaged because of the ink you
spilled on it. And your pencils need to
be sharpened for the drawing exam
tomorrow.'

'How do you know these things?'

'Because I am supposed to know everything that everyone is supposed to do. I am Yama,' said the man matter-of-factly.

'Ignore him, Jayshree,' said Kama. 'He is no fun.'

'She cannot
ignore me.
No one can.
I follow
everyone
everywhere.
People just
don't see me,'
said the man on
the buffalo.

'Because no one *wants*
to see you,' sneered
Kama.

'And no one *can* see
you,' retorted Yama.

'Leave this girl alone. She can see me.
I finally have a friend. And we want to

play or watch television or eat chips.
You are not invited,' shouted Kama.

'I don't need invitations. I will not
leave her. She has homework to do.
And having you around is not helping
her. You will make her forget her
responsibilities. You are no friend,'
said Yama, sounding rather superior.

Jayshree did not like Yama. But he did
speak the truth. She had homework
to do, but she was enjoying herself in
the garden. She had never seen such
flowers or smelt such perfumes and
she could not take her eyes off the
butterflies and parrots. Oh, what was
she to do?

'Let us go shopping,' said Kama. 'Let

me buy you a bright new
dress. Your clothes look so
boring.' Jayshree jumped
up excited. 'We can travel
on my parrot.'

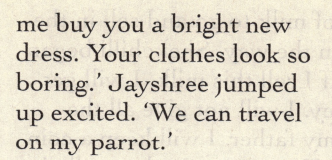

'See how he
distracts you,
Jayshree,' said
Yama. 'That is what he does.
That is why he was cursed
to become invisible.'

Jayshree wanted to
know more. So Yama
told the story of how
Kama came to be cursed.

Long ago, there was a young boy
called Shekchilli. His father gave

him a pot of milk to go and sell in the market. On the way, Shekchilli began to think. 'If I sell this milk, I will get some money. I will not give all the money to my father. I will keep a coin for myself. Tomorrow, Father will give me another pot of milk to sell. Again, I will not give him all the money. I will keep a coin for myself. In this way, I will collect many coins. When I have enough, I will buy a goat. The goat will give milk. I will sell the milk and make more money. The goat will have children. Some I will sell and some I will keep so that even they give me milk. All that milk I will sell and make a lot of money. I will use that money to buy a cow. The cow will give more milk and I will sell it to earn more money. When I have a lot of money, I

will buy a house. When I buy a house, I will get a wife. And my wife will cook food for me. And she will keep nagging me to come and eat. And I will shake my head and say, later, I will eat later, not now as I have work to do.' As Shekchilli kept daydreaming like this, he did not see a rock on the road. He stumbled on it and fell flat on the ground. The pot of milk on his head broke and all the milk was spilled. He was so angry that he cursed Kama, the god who makes you dream, to turn invisible.

'Hey, that is not correct,' said Kama. 'Shekchilli did not curse me.'

'Then who cursed you?' asked Jayshree.

'It was Shiva.'

Kama then told the story of how Shiva cursed him.

Shiva was a hermit who lived on Mount Kailash, which is covered with snow all year round. He wanted everyone to leave him alone. He was happy all by himself. He certainly did not want to marry. But Parvati, the princess of the mountains, wanted to marry him. She would travel to Mount Kailash every day and offer him fruits and flowers. Shiva would show no interest. He would keep his eyes firmly shut and not even bother to smile at the poor princess. Kama felt sorry for the princess and decided to help her. So he mounted his parrot and flew down to Mount Kailash. He picked up a flower and turned it into an arrow. He turned his shaft of sugar cane into a bow and requested the honey bees to fly in single line and serve as the bowstring. Thus he created a very special weapon that can make a man fall in love with a woman. Kama raised

the love bow
and shot the love
arrow at Shiva.
When Shiva was
shot at by the love
arrow he opened
his eyes and fell in
love with Parvati.
But something else
happened.
A third eye
appeared
on his
forehead
and out
came a
missile
of fire and its flames engulfed Kama.
And before Kama could say anything,
his body had been reduced to ashes.

Devdutt Pattanaik   227

Parvati was horrified. She begged
Shiva not to be so angry because
Kama was only trying to help. So
Shiva said, 'Kama will not die but he
will lose his body and stay invisible.'

'And did Shiva and Parvati marry?'
asked Jayshree.

'Of course they did. My arrows
never fail,' said Kama with a cheeky
smile. 'I even shot one at you so that you
stopped thinking of homework
and started thinking about television
and chips.'

'Aha, so you distracted me. You
made me dream. Turned me into a
Shekchilli.' Jayshree suddenly did
not like Kama as she did before.

'I told you that is what he does,'
said Yama.

Kama defended himself. 'If you do
only what is written in Yama's diary,
life will be boring. Imagine, if I had
not shot my arrow, Shiva would
have never opened his eyes and
Parvati, the poor princess of the
mountains, would have never got
married.'

'Nonsense. They were supposed to
marry. My diary said so. You should
not have interfered, ' said Yama. Yama's
buffalo nodded his head vigorously.

'If Yama had his way, everyone in
this world would be like Gangu Teli,'
said Kama.

'Who is Gangu Teli?' asked Jayshree.

Kama told her about Gangu Teli.
Gangu was a Teli, meaning a man who
makes oil. He had to press a bag full
of oilseeds in an oil-presser all day to

get one or two pots of oil. Pressing oil is a boring task. One has to go around rotating the presser all day. One can do nothing else all day. Just go round and round and round. No fun, just work and work and work.

'That is what Yama will make you—a Gangu Teli, pressing oil from oilseeds all day,' said Kama.

'I don't make oil,' clarified Jayshree.

'Oh, but you do homework. And you don't play and you don't have fun. Even your parents find you boring. Boring like Yama, just doing tasks and following his diary and never enjoying himself. You are no different from poor Gangu Teli.'

Yama defended himself. 'If Gangu Teli did not do what he was supposed to do, and spent his time daydreaming like Shekchilli, no one would get oil. What use is fun? It is just a waste of time. I feel every minute should be spent doing some work that helps the world. There is so much to do.'

Jayshree remembered something. She said, 'All work and no play makes Jack a dull boy. Gangu Teli is Jack.'

'Yes,' said Kama, glad that he had convinced Jayshree.

Yama retorted, 'All play and no work also make Jack a dull boy. Shekchilli is also Jack.'

Jayshree said, 'I don't want to be Shekchilli and I don't want to be Gangu Teli. I don't want to be either.'

'Then you will be Mitti ka Madho,' said both Yama and Kama. 'Or Gobar ki Gani.' They proceeded to explain what these two phrases meant.

Mitti means mud and Gobar means cowdung. A farmer was very unhappy because his children never listened to him. They never talked to him, and they never obeyed him. Frustrated, the farmer and his wife went to the temple and sought the help of the gods.

The farmer went to the Krishna temple and asked Krishna to give him a child who would always obey him.

The farmer's wife went to the Ganesha temple and also asked for a child who would always obey the farmer.

Krishna took some mud and created out of it a boy whose name was Mitti ka Madho. Ganesha took some cowdung and created out of it a

girl called Gobar ki Gani. 'Here you are,' said Krishna and Ganesha. 'Two children who will do nothing else but what you tell them to do.'

The farmer and his wife returned home with the boy and the girl, very happy to have two obedient children. But soon they realized that the children did nothing else but obey them. If they told the children to 'stand up', they stood up. If they told the children to 'sit down', they sat down. They never did anything on their own.

Once the farmer's wife told Mitti ka Madho, 'Go to the market and buy some sugar.' Madho went to the

market and bought sugar but did not return home. He kept waiting in the market because his mother had not told him to return home.

Another time the farmer told Gobar ki Gani, 'Go take a bath.' Gani took a bath but did not step out of the bathroom because her father had not told her so.

'Such stupid silly kids,' said Jayshree. 'They are useless!'

'The two children are neither Shekchilli nor Gangu Teli,' said Yama.

'You must be either Shekchilli or Gangu Teli,' said Kama.

'Choose my way—do what you are

supposed to do. Do your duties!' said Yama.

'Choose my way—do what you feel like. Have fun!' said Kama.

Jayshree did not know whom to choose. She loved doing homework. But sometimes she loved eating chips and watching television too.

She looked at Kama. He was so cute and charming with his colourful clothes, his sugar cane, his parrots, his bees and butterflies. He made her feel so happy and carefree. But he was so irresponsible. He did not care that his arrow caused Shekchilli to daydream and fall and break his pot and lose all his milk. Jayshree was

not sure if she liked Kama.

Jayshree then looked at Yama.
He looked so stern with his dull
clothes and his buffalo and his diary.
And he was so strict about doing
one's tasks.

Kama whispered in Jayshree's ears,
'Yama is the god of death. Surely,
you know. If you choose him, he will
kill you.'

Yama overheard Kama because his
ears are very sharp. He said, 'Being
the god of death is not a bad thing at
all. When you have done all that you
are supposed to do as per my diary,
you must leave the earth. It is my job
to help you leave the earth.'

'And where do we go?' asked Jayshree

'Across the river Vaitarni to the land of the dead,' answered Yama.

'And if I did not exist,' said Kama, 'everyone would stay in the land of dead. I bring people back into the land of the living.'

'Are you saying that I was once in the land of the dead? How come I don't remember?' asked Jayshree.

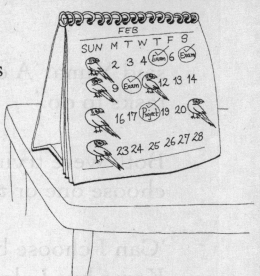

'The river Vaitarni takes away all memories,' said Yama. 'If I did not exist, all things would stay on earth and the earth would become a very crowded place.'

Jayshree looked at the garden, the trees, the flowers, the lotus pond and realized how beautiful it was, thanks to Kama. But if Yama did not exist, the flowers and the butterflies would stay in the garden forever. They would never go. Things would get boring.

'I am Sunday and all holidays,' said Kama. 'A day without rules and all fun.' 'I am Monday and all workdays,' said Yama. 'A day with rules and tasks to do.'

Both were trying hard to make her choose one or the other.

'Can I choose both of you? I love Kama but I also like Yama. I like doing homework but sometimes I would like to watch television and eat chips too,' said Jayshree.

'Of course you can,' said Kama.

'You will be like Raja Bhoj,' said Yama.

The gods then told Jayshree about Raja Bhoj. He was a wise king. For one half of the month, from new moon

to full moon, when the moon would wax, he would sit in court, and do everything a ruler is supposed to do — building roads and solving problems and settling disputes. For the other half of the month, from full moon to new moon, when the moon wanes, he would spend time playing with his wife and children, listening to music and watching dance performances, swimming in the river or riding on elephants in the forest.

'He balanced Kama and Yama,' exclaimed Jayshree. 'Yes, I want to be Raja Bhoj.'

'So you will be,' said the two gods.

Kama then rose to the sky on his

parrot, waved his sugar cane and flew
towards the east. Yama nodded his
head, tapped his diary and got on to
his buffalo to walk towards the west.

Kama vs Yama

Jayshree found herself all alone in the garden.

She took a decision. 'First I will finish my homework. Then I will watch television and eat chips.' It felt good to be Raja Bhoj.

Gauri
and the
Talking Cow

Gauri was convinced that milk came from packets that she and her father picked up every Saturday morning from the supermarket near her house. The supermarket had rows of shelves and each shelf had rows of racks and each rack had boxes of many colours. Each box contained a different type of milk—toned milk, skimmed milk, standard milk, low fat milk…

Imagine Gauri's surprise when she visited a farmhouse and discovered that milk comes from animals called cows!

One Saturday, Gauri's parents decided to visit a friend who lived in a farm located just outside the city. It was a beautiful place, with many trees, each one a different shade of green, some bearing fruits and some bearing flowers. There were ducks in the pond, and goats in the front yard, and two

dogs who ran all around the house.
But the most wonderful sight was that
of a big black cow in an open shed
located next to the backyard.

Gauri saw a man bending under the
cow and squeezing out milk. 'Does
that hurt?' Gauri asked.

'Not really,' said the cow. 'This man is taking my milk so that you can drink it later. This is fresh milk and tastes much better than the stuff you drink from packets.'

Gauri had never seen a talking cow. She never knew that cows could talk! The cow said, 'Generally we don't talk.

But today I am in the mood. I like your name, Gauri. Do you know Gauri is the name of a goddess?'

Gauri shook her head. So the cow decided to tell her the story of the goddess called Gauri.

Once there was a goddess in the forest. Her name was Kali, meaning the dark one. She had thick black hair that she never combed or oiled. Her hair was long and stretched out behind her like the tail of a peacock. And when it was windy they rose up to reach the sky, surrounding her face. It all looked scary.

Everyone was scared of Kali. She reminded them of a dense forest full of

creepers and vines and wild animals
and ghosts. But no one told Kali
that she was scary, because she was
a goddess and you do not tell such
things to a goddess. You are afraid she
might get angry. And an angry goddess
is worse than a scary goddess.

One day, however, a little girl saw this
goddess. Then she said, 'Oh look, there
is Kali with her long hair blowing in the
breeze. She is truly as scary as they say.'

Kali did not like what the little girl
said. She realized it was the truth.
People were scared of the way she
looked. 'What should I do?' Kali asked
the little girl.

'It will help if you oiled your hair and

combed your hair, the way I do.'
Kali thought it was good advice. So
she oiled her hair, and combed it and
tied it in a neat bun and decorated it
with flowers. She now looked very
beautiful. Everyone called her Gauri,
the radiant one.

'There are days I do not want to oil or comb my hair. On those days, they can call me Kali. But on days my hair is in order, they can call me Gauri,' the goddess said.

Everyone realized that Kali and Gauri are the same. Mothers told their daughters, 'Kali is the forest. She is wild. Gauri is the garden. She is domestic. Kali stays outside the house. Gauri comes inside the house. That is why what is outside is scary and what is inside is not.'

Gauri liked this story. She clapped her hands. 'But I don't like to oil my hair or comb my hair,' she told the cow. 'Maybe I should call myself Kali.'

'Do you want to scare people?' asked the cow, sounding a bit concerned.

'No, but it would be nice if people were a little afraid of me.'

'You are a silly girl. Now go and get me some grass. That is the least you can do if you are going to drink my milk.'

Gauri picked up a bunch of grass from a tray nearby and gave it to the cow. 'What is your name?' she asked. The cow swallowed the grass quickly and then answered, 'Sweety.'

'Why Sweety?'

'Because my milk is sweet.'

'You should be called Kali-Gauri

because you are black and white in colour.'

'I think my sweet milk matters more than my colour, don't you think?'

Gauri saw a twinkle in Sweety's eye. Oh, she loved this talking cow! She hugged Sweety, who made a sound of satisfaction indicating she liked the hug.

'Who is the man who takes milk out of your body?' asked Gauri.

'He is my cowherd. He feeds me, bathes me, takes care of me. He cleans my shed too. Why don't you rub your hands across my back like he does? I like that. And why don't you help him clean the shed?'

Gauri noticed that the far end of the shed was full of cowdung and cow urine. It was disgusting. She made a face. 'Can't you use a toilet?' she asked the cow.

'No. I cannot and will not. Toilets are for human beings. Animals do not use

toilets. Did you know that my dung
can be used as fuel and my urine was
once used as medicine?'

There was so much Gauri did not
know. So Sweety, the cow, decided to
enlighten Gauri.

She told Gauri that Brahma created
the first cow. Her name was Surabhi.
She was also called Nandini. She was
given to wise men known as rishis.
Rishis drank her milk. They also
turned the milk into curds and butter
and ghee and cheese.

Surabhi's dung was used to make dung-
cakes that served as fuel. In the olden

days, they did not have piped gas or gas cylinders, so women burned dung-cakes to cook food. They still do so today in villages. Cooking using dung takes a long time as the flame is very gentle unlike the fiery leaping flames that one gets by burning wood and straw.

The dung was also mixed with straw and used to plaster the floor and

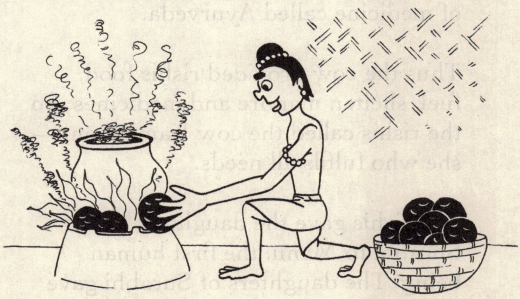

houses. It kept certain insects out of the house and filled the house with a gentle fragrance. The dung also served as manure. It was scattered on the fields after harvest to help the earth regain its health.

The urine was thought to have medicinal properties and was used by doctors who followed a system of medicine called Ayurveda.

Thus the cow provided rishis food, fuel, shelter, manure and medicines. So the rishis called the cow Kamadhenu — she who fulfils all needs.

The rishis gave the daughters of Surabhi to Manu, the first human being. The daughters of Surabhi gave

milk and dung and urine to man.
The children of Manu were so happy
that they decided to worship cows
as a goddess.

'Guess what they called her?' asked
Sweety.

'How would I know?' said Gauri.

'They called her Gauri. Gau or Go means cow.'

'Why were cows not called Kali?'

'Because cows are gentle and domestic and hurt no man. Kali is the tiger, wild and free and scary like the forest.'

Sweety had many more things to tell Gauri about cows.

Those who took care of cows were called Gopas. They were the cowherds. They took her to graze in pastures, bathed her and watched over her. The most famous cowherd was, of course, Krishna. He would play the

flute to entertain the cows. He was also called Govind and Gopal.

Krishna protected the cows from various calamities. Once, when a fire broke out in the forest, he swallowed the fire and protected the cows.

Another time, Krishna noticed that the cows were afraid of bathing in the river Yamuna because its waters had been polluted by a terrible serpent called Kaliya. Krishna danced on the hood of Kaliya until he promised to go away.

'Krishna still takes care of cows in a heaven called Go-loka,' said Sweety. 'It is said that whenever human beings treat the earth badly, she takes the form of a cow and begs Krishna to come to her rescue.'

'Why would anyone treat the earth badly? The earth gives us everything,' said Gauri.

Sweety replied, 'Of all the animals in the world, only humans destroy

nature in order to build their houses,
roads, fields and industries. When
this destruction of nature becomes too
much, then the earth takes the form of
a cow and begs Krishna for help. Once
the earth got so angry with human
beings that she refused to let the grass

grow and the trees bear flower or fruit. After much persuasion, Krishna was able to calm her down and she allowed the grass to grow and the trees to bear flower and fruit.'

Gauri was excited. She suddenly realized why the earth takes the form of a cow to meet Krishna. She said, 'The earth is like a cow. If we take care of her, she will give us milk in the form of plants and fruits and flowers. If we do not take care of her, she will stop giving us milk. We have to be like cowherds who take care of the cow. We have to be cowherds of the earth. Like Krishna!'

'Well said, my girl,' said Sweety. 'Did you know that in ancient times the gift of a cow was considered the greatest gift?'

'Why?' asked Gauri.

'Because when you gave a cow to a man, you gave him a source of food and fuel. All his needs were met and he could think of other things besides trying to earn a living. He could think of maybe becoming an artist or a musician or a poet. He did not have to wonder where his next meal would come from.'

'What a wonderful idea! Do people still give cows to people?'

'Some do. Though now it means giving a person a job, so he has the money to buy things. Imagine if your father did not have a job. He would not have money to buy you milk from the supermarket every Saturday.'

Gauri was suddenly sad and scared when she heard this.

Sweety said, 'Oh don't be sad. Cows need grass. Trees need water. Pigeons need grain. Humans need money. For money one needs to do a job. In the olden days, instead of money, people were paid with cows for their services.'

The talking cow then told Gauri the story of a king called Indradyumna.

Once upon a time, there was a king called Indradyumna. He did many good deeds in his life. And so, after

Gauri and the Talking Cow

he died, he was invited to stay in
paradise along with the gods. There
he lived for many years surrounded by
joyful things. But then, one day, the
gods said, 'Indradyumna, you have to
go back to earth. You are no longer
welcome in paradise.'

'Why?' asked a perplexed Indradyumna.

'Because,' said the gods, 'no one on earth remembers your good deeds.'

'But how can that be?' wondered the king. 'I spent all my life doing good deeds.'

'If you can find at least one creature who remembers you for your good deeds, you can come back to heaven. Otherwise you will have to leave. That is the rule,' said the gods.

Time flows differently on earth where humans live than in paradise where gods live. When Indradyumna reached earth, he realized that centuries had passed since his reign. The trees were different, people were different, even his kingdom looked different.

The temples and buildings he built were all gone. The people to whom he gave cows were all dead. No one he met remembered any king called Indradyumna.

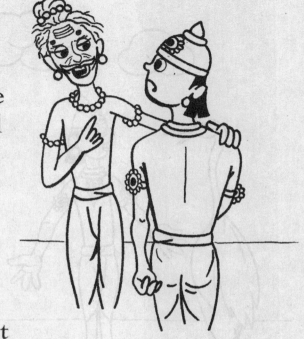

Disheartened, Indradyumna went in search of the oldest man on earth. He found Rishi Markandeya. But the rishi did not remember him. 'There is an owl who is older than me,' said the sage. 'Go to him.'

Indradyumna did so. He found the owl and asked him, 'Do you remember

King Indradyumna?'

The owl said, 'No, I do not remember such a king but ask the stork who is older than me.'

Even the stork did not remember. 'But I know someone who is much older than me, who may know of King Indradyumna,' said the stork. 'He is an old tortoise who lives in a lake.'

Indradyumna went to the tortoise
who was very old and slow and
tired. To Indradyumna's great relief,
he did remember a king called
Indradyumna. 'He built this lake,'
said the tortoise.

'But I never built this lake,' said Indradyumna, rather bewildered by this piece of information. 'This lake did not even exist when I was king.'

The tortoise explained, 'My grandfather never lied. He told me that this king spent his entire life

giving cows in charity, hundreds of thousands of cows.'

Indradyumna recollected that he had. He had been told that gifting cows assures one a place in heaven. But now where were his cows? Where were the people to whom he gave the cows?

The tortoise continued, 'As these cows left Indradyumna's city, they kicked up so much dust it created a large hole in the ground. When the rains came, water collected in this hole and turned it into a lake. Now that lake provides sustenance to innumerable plants and animals and worms and weeds and fish and turtles and birds. So we remember the great King Indradyumna, whose act of

charity resulted in a lake which for generations has been our home.'

Indradyumna was pleased to hear what the tortoise had to say. So were the gods who welcomed him back.

'I love this story!' said Gauri.

'It is a good story. I am happy every time I narrate it,' said Sweety. 'Imagine, the king is remembered for things he did not even realize he had done. We often do not realize the good things we

do. But the same thing holds true for bad things,' warned Sweety.

Gauri was puzzled by Sweety's remark. What did she mean? So Sweety decided to tell Gauri the story of Nruga.

Once there was a king, just like Indradyumna, who loved giving cows away as gifts. His name was Nruga. One day, Nruga gave a cow to a priest.

The cow given was young and rather mischievous. She ran away. The priest was old and could not run fast enough to catch her.

The cow returned to the royal cowshed; it was the only home she knew.

Nruga then gave the same cow as a gift to a philosopher, not realizing that he had already given her earlier that day to the old priest. The philosopher was young and strong and he ensured that the cow did not run away from him, even though she tried.

The old priest saw the cow with the young philosopher. 'Hey you,' said the priest, 'where are you taking my cow?'

'Your cow?' replied the philosopher. 'She is my cow. King Nruga just gave her to me.'

'He would never do that,' said the priest. 'He just gave her to me earlier today.'

The philosopher shouted, 'You are a

liar. This is my cow, a gift from Nruga.'

The priest shouted back, 'You are a thief. This is my cow, a gift from Nruga.'

Now people gathered around to find out what was happening. Both the

priest and the philosopher insisted
that the cow belonged to them. Both
insisted that King Nruga had given
them the cow. The only way to resolve
the situation was to go to the king.

Gauri and the Talking Cow

Nruga looked at the priest, the philosopher and the cow. He realized he had, without realizing it, given the same cow to two people. 'I made a terrible mistake. I apologize. I am responsible for this confusion. Let me make it up to you. Let me give both of you two cows.'

'What about this cow?' said the priest.

Nruga did not know what to do. 'I cannot duplicate the cow. I cannot divide the cow between two people. What can I do?'

The priest and philosopher were angry with the king. They both cursed the king. As a result, after King Nruga died, he was reborn as a lizard.

'What a terrible story. What happened to the lizard?' asked Gauri.

Sweety said, 'Krishna took pity on him and released him from the curse.'

'I think the priest and the philosopher should have forgiven the king. People make mistakes,' said Gauri.

'My dear, it is not easy to forgive people. Look at the earth. She forgives human beings all the time and yet human beings treat her badly.'

'I will never treat the earth badly,' swore Gauri.

'You are a lovely girl,' said Sweety.

Gauri gave Sweety some more grass.
Sweety was sure Gauri would enjoy
her sweet milk. A lizard ran across the
shed towards the goats. Gauri looked
at Sweety. Both laughed.